A New ME:

Looking to the future

Barry John Evans

Copyright © 2014 Barry John Evans

All rights reserved.

ISBN-13: 978-1499585490
ISBN-10: 1499585497

Dedication

First of all, I would like to dedicate this book to any M.E. sufferers. We are one big family who feel like the world is against us. I have received so much support from support groups and thank every single sufferer who has been there for me.

Second of all, I would like to dedicate this book to my mum. She's always been there for me and has been incredibly supportive. Life would have been a lot harder without her support.

Last of all, I would like to dedicate this book to my church family. Ever since I was small they've been there for me whether I've been attending regularly or not. It's very comforting to know that I have the support of these people.

Contents

1. Let's Get Our Facts straight - 9

2. The Early Years - 23

3. Leading up to an M.E. Diagnosis - 55

4. My First Year with M.E. - 71

5. Looking to the Future – 123

Chapter 1: Let's get our Facts straight

Dear reader, thank you for taking the time to read my book. First of all, I'd like to explain my reasoning behind the cover art. The butterfly represents a new beginning and the idea is that it stands out against the rest of the picture. The contrast in colors I felt worked well also.

Now I'm going to introduce myself:

I was born Barry John Evans on the 8th April 1991 making me aged 23 at the time of writing this book.

I was born and raised in a little seaside town in the North West of England called Southport.

I was diagnosed with Asperger Syndrome aged nine.

I graduated from university in 2012 and also from a Personal Training academy.

I was diagnosed with Myalgic Encephalomyelitis on the 10th January 2013.

I have gone from mild to moderate in a short space of time and have since had to adapt my life to accommodate this.

So why am I writing this book?

The reason I have decided to write this book is for a number of reasons.

Firstly, M.E. is a chronic illness and I want to do as much as I possibly can to raise awareness for it and help those who are suffering, especially those who are severe. Secondly, I feel my story can be related to, not only by M.E. sufferers and people who care for them, but also by those with Autism and those who look after those with the condition too.

Lastly, it's a way for me to close the lid on the past and to show there's hope for those who can relate to my story. That's why you will see no past pictures of me in the book. There will also be no names mentioned for this reason and also because I don't want to isolate anybody.

I also feel that it's very important to keep a positive outlook on life despite suffering and I'm hoping you will see that, especially in the last chapter of this book.

Also, 10% of sales made online from this book will be going to the charity Invest in ME. I have chosen to do this over an Autism charity due to the reasons above. Asperger Syndrome doesn't lack awareness like M.E. does and it isn't fatal whilst M.E. can be.

I'm now going to show you why I have chosen this particular charity:

> *Invest in ME (LiME) was set up with the objectives of making a change in how ME is perceived and treated in the media, by health departments and by healthcare professionals*

They later go on to state that the three key areas they're looking at are biomedical research, education and lobbying.

Before moving onto my story, I would like to present to you a few facts about Myalgic Encephalomyelitis and also about Asperger Syndrome. The reason I am doing this is so you gain a better basic understanding of the two making my story more understandable.

So what is M.E.?

I'm going to use the description used on the Invest in ME Awareness Leaflet as I feel it gives a very thorough and descriptive insight into what M.E. actually is.

> *ME is a severely debilitating neurological illness.*
>
> *It has distinct: onset; symptoms; causes; responses; and, long and short term prognoses. ME is an acquired illness with multi system involvement which is characterized by post encephalitic damage to the brain, brain stem and the Central Nervous System (CNS).*

Reaction to physical and mental activity and sensory input is unique to ME. Over-exertion can make ME worse and the effects are often delayed and may not be seen within 24 hours.

Symptoms can range from mild to severe to life-threatening and can include:

- *Cardiac and Cardiovascular Problems*
- *Cognitive Dysfunction*
- *Gastro-intestinal Problems*
- *Headaches*
- *Hormonal Imbalance*
- *Immunological Problems*
- *Muscle Weakness and Intense Pain*
- *Neurological Problems*
- *Sleep Problems*

For me personally, the fatigue has hit me most. Every day I feel energy less, particularly in the mornings. This is when I'm most painful, mainly in the limbs, whilst my eyes feel like they've been sand papered and my joints feel stiff and achy. It's an indescribable pain that feels like no other. Maybe a little like the aches you feel when you get the flu but with more of a throbbing sensation. I always leave the house with some form a mobility aid, my balance is terrible and indoors I find it easier to lean on things.

The cognitive problems are overwhelming, you can't think straight however hard you try and become more fatigued the more you try to concentrate.

Spending an hour outside the house usually means the next day is spent mostly lying down with the aches and fatigue worse.

I wear my tinted glasses/ sun glasses the majority of the time as light often makes my sight blurry and gives me headaches.

My body is more intolerable to certain foods so my diet has to stay strict.

I get small heart palpitations too, usually after over-exerting myself. Over-exerting can be something as little as going out to buy a loaf of bread. I've had to cut down my activity by at least 75% meaning I have to spend my time wisely.

Stress levels can increase the symptoms significantly though the M.E. is what can cause a lot of stress in the first place, it can be a vicious circle.

Yet no-one can see I'm experiencing these things because it's invisible. What could I possibly gain from sacrificing so much? It's isolated me incredibly. I'm not lazy, I'm ill. More doctors are starting to believe but still nowhere near as many as there should be. It's a horrible illness and one of the biggest worries of all is the stress of trying to get friends and family to believe you. It's crippling in many ways and has turned my life upside down.

Now you have a pretty good insight into what M.E. is, I would like to describe to you what Asperger Syndrome is. That way, you can see how the two together can affect someone.

I have decided to use The National Autistic Society's description as I feel it's very thorough and descriptive.

> *Asperger syndrome is a form of autism, which is a lifelong disability that affects how a person makes sense of the world, processes information and relates to other people. Autism is often described as a 'spectrum disorder' because the condition affects people in many different ways and to varying degrees.*
>
> *Asperger syndrome is mostly a 'hidden disability'. This means that you can't tell that someone has the condition from their outward appearance. People with the condition have difficulties in three main areas. They are:*

- *Social communication*
- *Social interaction*
- *Social imagination*

It later goes on to state the problems within these three main areas.

Difficulty with social communication

- *Have difficulty understanding gestures, facial expressions or tone of voice*
- *Have difficulty knowing when to start or end a conversation and choosing topics to talk about*
- *Use complex words and phrases but may not fully understand what they mean*

- *Be very literal in what they say and can have difficulty understanding jokes, metaphor and sarcasm. For example, a person with Asperger Syndrome may be confused by the phrase 'That's cool' when people use it to say something is good*

Difficulty with social interaction

- *Struggle to make and maintain friendships*
- *Not understand the unwritten 'social rules' that most of us pick up without thinking. For example, they may stand too close to another person, or start an inappropriate topic of conversation*
- *Find other people unpredictable and confusing*
- *Become withdrawn and seem uninterested in other people, appearing almost aloof*
- *Behave in what may seem an inappropriate manner*

Difficulty with social imagination

- *Imagining alternative outcomes to situations and finding it hard to predict what will happen next*
- *Understanding or interpreting other people's thoughts, feelings or actions. The subtle messages that are put across by facial expression and body language are often missed*
- *Having a limited range of imaginative activities, which can be pursued rigidly and repetitively, eg lining up toys or collecting and organizing things related to his or her interest*

Lastly, the characteristics of Asperger Syndrome include:

- *Love of routines*
- *Special interests*
- *Sensory difficulties*

My Asperger Syndrome has improved over the years as I've learnt how to deal with each characteristic appropriately. Many don't realize I have this as I can be good at covering it up and it is only a mild form. However, it has affected me greatly over the years with particular regard to my childhood. Social activity has always been incredibly difficult for me, I can appear expressionless and unfriendly when in reality I feel the complete opposite inside.

My love of routines has had to be adapted as my M.E. makes it very hard to stick to it so I try to set smaller routines like eating the same meals on particular nights or making sure I get twenty minutes singing practice in.

Special interests have helped me to focus my interests away from people and appearing obsessive. I was a massive wrestling fan growing up, I then became a massive fan of football and the gym in high school and now I am a massive fan of music.

Things like statistics fascinate me and it has been known to be common amongst those with Asperger's that figures are a strong point. With wrestling, the heights and weights of wrestlers really took my interest, football scores with football and now vocal ranges with singers.

I hope that now you have a better understanding of both M.E. and also Asperger Syndrome. I also hope that it helps you to understand my story more than you may have done without the knowledge of these.

Chapter 2: The Early Years

I was born on 8th April 1991. My parents noticed odd patterns in my behaviour as a child and at the age of nine diagnosed with Asperger Syndrome. I really struggled to make friends at school, I went to 3 different primary schools and I hated each one more than the last. The last primary school I went to I started in year 3 and stayed until I left. It felt like torture and I hated it with a passion. I was the kid that everybody picked on just to jump on the bandwagon. I was mentally bullied every single day and sometimes it was physical. At one point, I couldn't even walk to school without being pushed around by a few lads. The bullying had mentally scarred me. It was the bullying inside of school that was worse, several complaints were made to the teachers but very little was ever done. The daily bullying is what turned me into a very mentally weak and extremely quiet individual. I pulled out every trick in the book trying to make myself ill just so I didn't have to go in and suffer more humiliation.

My parents split up around this time but I wanted them to stay together. They argued daily but this felt normal to me, anything was better than life at school.

I was into American Wrestling and spent the majority of my time watching old video tapes; it was an escape from reality. I wished that I could be like the guys I was watching on T.V.

My childhood is an experience I have very few good memories of, it's a phase in my life that I never reflect upon. I destroyed all the evidence I had of my childhood. One not so fond memory I have is when a Rottweiler dog ripped a chunk of my hand off at a friend's birthday party, I got the whole birthday cake but I'd rather have had a healthy hand to be honest.

There's a mental blockage and I never look back on photos as they bring back unhappy memories.

High school was a slight improvement in some ways. I had fewer "friends" but the bullying had improved. All in all, I had very few happy memories and the bad memories far outweighed the happy ones. I spent more lunchtimes on my own than I would have liked and did whatever I could to try and get a day off school. I felt like I was the ugliest kid in the year and was always thinking of ways I could try to alter my appearance as it was really bothering me, I felt like a spotty alien.

In the last few years of school I had a mentor; they helped me greatly and introduced me to a Youth Group they were involved in. I wasn't keen on the idea but went along after some persuasion and became more involved in that.

At 14 I decided I wanted to join a gym. I was tall, skinny, had bad acne and wanted get bigger in the hope that the bully's would back off. I grew to love working out and at one point was going to the gym seven days a week.

I was also involved in a local football team for a couple of seasons playing as a defender; I really enjoyed playing but felt uncomfortable around many of my team mates, I ignored a lot of the jibes and tried to focus purely on the football. I love football and regularly played at a local field for hours after school, often as a goalkeeper because I loved playing in goal too even though I managed to break 3 different fingers in the space of a few months.

I was always very sporty but didn't often partake in P.E. lessons at school as people made fun of the way I ran. I also used to wear shoes a size too small as they made fun of the size of my feet and as a result have very crooked toes.

Outside of school I loved playing others sports such as tennis and used to enjoy cycling and running too.

I didn't try very hard in my GCSE exams. I had to take them in a room upstairs with a few other pupils to accommodate my Aspergers. I managed to get seven GCSE's or equivalents in Business Studies, Graphic Design and Science. I then went on to get equivalents in Maths and I.T. at college.

I left school in June 2007, I was relieved. It's a common saying that the best years of your life are your school years but in my case they were the worst. I hated it and felt free once I had left. The distraction of school no longer existing had made me soon realize how very few friends I actually had.

Throughout the summer of 2007, there was one friend I kept in touch with regularly but the rest of the time I was mainly a loner. This was the friend who would later cut contact with me. Committing crime became the norm and at the time I enjoyed it, it was an escape from true reality.

I went to Macedonia with the Youth Club, it was a once in a lifetime opportunity but my depression had blinded me. I didn't make the most of the experience; I was very socially awkward so making friends with people from another culture was a daunting prospect. The place was gorgeous and the people were very friendly. The people I was with were very good with me, I wasn't the easiest person to understand but they handled me very well. I felt totally out of it which was probably by my own doing and I can imagine that I came across as very moody at times.

My mind wasn't in the right place. The Macedonians came back to Southport a month later. One evening we were in or around Oldham (if I remember correctly) and went to a nightclub like place. I had pre-judgments and didn't want to go in. That evening I spent mostly alone and it was time to reflect, I was different from everybody else and hated everything about me.

I had college lined up in September but wasn't really looking forward to it. I started to feel very depressed and felt the world was against me.

I always dreaded first days at school and the same applied for college. I was going to study a National Diploma in Public Services. I was quite keen on the idea of becoming a Policeman or a Prison Guard which was quite ironic considering the way I spent the summer. I remember the first day was a teambuilding day, we participated in water sports. I worked myself up so much that I made myself ill; I was shaking and lost my appetite because I was frightened about meeting more people. I considered suicide that night, that's how bad I felt, it was a buildup of everything and I didn't know how I was going to cope.

I'd been to see my GP and saw my first psychiatrist in October. They prescribed me Fluoxetine. I was pleased that something was being done but I felt the line of questioning wasn't thorough enough though I wasn't complaining.

I got on with the majority of people in my class but never really got close to anyone. People had formed their friendships and I felt I was being left out. I knew that they thought I was a weirdo. We were thinking of words to describe each other and "sleepy" were the definite word for me. Little did I know it would be nothing compared to the fatigue I'm experiencing now.

I'd arranged a few photo shoots in the hope it would build my confidence up. However, I began to feel more depressed as time went by. I wasn't enjoying the course and I didn't enjoy the trips either, I was just waiting for home time every day.

The Christmas holidays had arrived and in one sense I was relieved though I knew they would be spent at home. I wanted to be with friends, they just didn't exist. In the last week before going back to college, I began to get incredibly worked up again and didn't want to go back. I hated spending lunchtimes alone trying to find things to do. Even one of the teachers made a joke at me because of my lack of expression. It wasn't my fault I had Asperger's, the whole class laughed and it really upset me. I was very sensitive to negative comments. It wasn't much as a surprise really, an old Science teacher at school pretended to pop a spot as a jibe at the fact I had acne.

It was in the January of 2008 that I'd finally had enough. I overdosed on a month's supply of anti-depressants in the hope to end my life. The original plan was to neck a bottle of vodka whole though luckily I wasn't able to get hold of one. I remember feeling guilty towards my mum straight after the overdose. After all, she was the one who had always supported me. It was within 5 minutes of the overdose that I confessed to her. I thought she'd be annoyed but she was more upset. Straight away she called my dad and he picked me up to take me to hospital. I felt bloated and little did I know that the medication I overdosed on wasn't enough to end the misery.

I was put on a drip to drain all of the medication out of my body. I was also told that I'd be seeing a psychiatrist as soon as possible.

The first night I was there, I sent a text to my supposed best friend. I didn't hear back and they started ignoring my calls. It was only a few months later from an acquaintance that I found out they'd said something along the lines of "I've tried to make him happy, if he's going to do that then what's the point in being friends with him?!" It was a horrible feeling; the one friend I trusted had turned their back on me.

I began to get used to hospital life. A television, a CD player, and most of all, no-one who negatively judged me. What more could I possibly want?!

I did have a few visits though mainly from people from church. I received a phone call from a friend whilst I was there. They asked me if I wanted to go halves on a bag of weed. I told them what had happened and I didn't hear from them again. That just about summed up the quality of my friendships at that time.

It was almost a week after I'd been in hospital that I saw a psychiatrist. They asked me lots of questions. I found it easier answering questions than trying to explain everything that was going on in my head. This was the first psychiatrist I really took to. I hoped to see them again but later found out they had flown out to the Caribbean later that week. Was I really that bad?!

It was approaching a week when I was told that I'd be discharged from hospital. I was disappointed. I remember returning home that day feeling depressed. It was the worst I'd felt in the whole of the past week. I preferred life in hospital.

I had been prescribed Sertraline in the hope that my depression could be kept under control. After a few weeks of staying in bed, I returned to college. I'd missed over a month's lectures so had to drop down a class. Not only was it a daunting prospect returning to college, I was returning to a class full of people I'd never met before.

I'd made a few friends but it took me a while to settle in. I was now studying for a National Certificate instead of a National Diploma. I was just happy that the workload had lessened slightly and it wouldn't take me as long to catch up.

During this time, I had the Crisis Prevention and Response Team keeping an eye on me. They used to visit me once a week. My mum had to hide away my medication as I was deemed a risk to myself. I couldn't be left alone for a long period of time. I felt trapped and kept it very secret as I didn't want others to know I was seeing them, I had no choice in the matter.

After a while of visiting the house, we used to go out for coffees and play snooker. It did me good at the time even though I couldn't see how it was helping me.

I was also seeing someone from the Leisure Inclusion team; they said they could be my

Personal Trainer which I was chuffed about. They ran in competitions and I used to go out on runs, I couldn't keep up with them though I could lift more in the weights room.

We stayed in touch after I had officially stopped seeing them. I really looked up to and enjoyed spending my time with them. We went mountain biking in Wales, I flew off and fell shoulder first into a ditch. It was badly bruised so the biking was cut short. They dropped me off at the train station 30 minutes away from Southport and I had to carry my bags home with a badly bruised shoulder. I very quickly lost touch and was devastated that yet another "friend" had betrayed me. They were great at the time but I was very disappointed with how it all ended. After all, I had done nothing wrong. I was in a sling for a while and had problems with my shoulder at the gym for a few years after that.

However, there were a couple of positives to take from meeting with the different teams. I was introduced to a Drama Class

and also told about a Wrestling School which I did my research on.
I didn't have the confidence to be a part of the Drama Class. The whole point of joining was to boost my confidence but I was so out of my comfort zone. We were meant to be performing in a Christmas play but I bottled it just days before. I had worked myself up so much about it that I made myself ill.

The Wrestling School however was a dream of mine. I was nervous but really wanted to go along and experience what it was like to be a wrestler. I made the phone call and went along the following Saturday. It was expensive for me at the time at £25 per lesson though it was a for a full day. There were around ten of us and we started out by doing some pretty intense stretches. We then "conditioned" the body by throwing ourselves to the mats making sure all our body parts were in the right place. Little things like having your hands facing down made all the difference. I found it fascinating. I was the new guy and it was tough but I really wanted to stick at it. At the end of the lesson we had a Tag Match. It was an opportunity for me to get used to the ring. I loved it. That evening, we all went to see a show that some of the students were taking part in, we saw the ring being set up and met a few of the guys who were wrestling. My body ached all over on the Sunday's but nothing compared to the aches I get now. It was a good ache and more than bearable.

I lasted around six weeks before I stopped going, I didn't have enough money to attend and my workload at college was increasing by the minute. I always planned on going back but unfortunately it never happened. It saddens me that I may never get the opportunity again but health always comes first.

I was going on weekly trips with the college class and went skiing, camping and hiking amongst other activities. Around this time my psychiatrist had prescribed me Venlafaxine as the Sertraline wasn't working. I didn't make the most of the trips and the stress was mounting up knowing how much work I had to do.

The last couple of weeks at college had arrived and I had to complete half a year's work. It seemed impossible but somehow I managed to get through it. I wasn't bothered about the marks as I just wanted to pass.

I'd also been diagnosed with what is called Irlen Syndrome around this time. It affects the way the brain processes information visually and is a perceptual problem. I found reading black writing on white paper difficult. Someone I saw regularly from Student Services diagnosed me and suggested I went to see someone to get tinted glasses made; the only place was in Macclesfield a fair way from me.

There's a screening to determine whether someone has the condition or not. It's a visual test and mentally draining. I had to read the same paragraph over and over using different colored filters. It turned out that rose was the color best for me. Little help was available for this and so it cost

£300 just to get my rose tinted lenses. I still use the lenses to this day, they're great and I find I have to use them a lot more now than I used to, it helps with the sensitivity to light I have.

The summer of 2009 had arrived and I didn't have a clue what I wanted to do with my life. I thought about applying to the Police Force or to the Prison Service, I felt that my medical history would hold me back and so never applied. Luckily I had made a couple of new friends as I saw my college friends less and less as contact was gradually decreasing.

To boost my confidence up, I'd become quite involved in modeling. I became to enjoy it; it made me feel good about myself. I enjoyed dressing up for the different styles and wearing the different sorts of make-up. It was a way I could express myself without being judged. I travelled around to a few locations around the North West and met some great people through it. Though there was one embarrassing moment when I was asked by a fellow model to go to an audition in Leeds to be involved in a catwalk. I literally did no research whatsoever and just turned up not having a clue what I was going to be doing. It's safe to say that I never heard back after completing the audition.

I also met one of my musical inspirations, Rhydian. I'd followed him ever since he was on the x-factor and was a big fan of his style. Great voice and flamboyant too. It was after one of his concerts in Liverpool that I had a good 5-10 minute chat with him. It was great to speak to him and I always remember him telling me I had the image of a pop star. I told him he'd inspired me to look into getting singing lessons, little did he know it would take me four years after that to finally make the move.

I started working as a Painter/Decorator which for parts I enjoyed. There was a satisfaction about seeing the end result though the days were long and exhausting. It wasn't something I ever saw myself doing for the rest of my career but I stuck at it.

The money was good and at the time was just what I needed. However, it suddenly struck me towards the end of that summer that I wasn't aiming towards anything. I arranged an interview at the college I had been at for the past two years and asked if I could enroll for a further two years on a Business course. The person I saw was very helpful and suggested I apply at University. They said it would be a sideways step if I went back to college.

That week I did some online research looking into Foundation Degrees. I hadn't a clue what they were and wasn't really sure if I wanted to commit myself to another few years of study. There were 2 places left at colleges in Kirkby and Runcorn. Runcorn wasn't a realistic option considering I had to rely on public transport and Kirkby involved 4 train journeys a day. I decided that I would ring the college in Kirkby and they said there was only one place left on the course, I jumped at it. I didn't really take the travel into consideration as I knew I'd left it too late to look at any other possible alternatives.

The days involved me arising at 6.30am, a 20 minute walk to the train station, a 40 minute train ride followed by a 15 minute train ride, a 10 minute walk from the station to the college and then repeat the same sequence going home. They were long days; I always slept on the train as I found it hard staying awake. When I got home the first thing I would do is sleep for around 2 hours before having something to eat. I was doing this, whilst working as a Painter/Decorator a couple of times a week. It was tough but I kept it up.

In October 2009, I also started working at a Holiday Camp serving fast food. It wasn't really my scene and I wasn't overly keen on the idea of serving swingers meal deals at 3am every morning. Contracts were only handed out per season and I decided not to renew my contract after it had run out over a month later. The last shift I worked started at 9pm and lasted all the way through till 9am the next day; it drained me physically and mentally having to be in college the next day. I never wanted to smell chips and fries again though I don't think the dogs forgave me as I wasn't regularly bringing home boxes of popcorn chicken for them.

I'd had enough of studying but in the end was persuaded to stick with it. Problems were mounting up as personal relationships had turned very sour and I found myself in some very dicey situations. I couldn't focus on my work and felt no real connection with my classmates. In the middle of all this, my anti-depressants dosage was increased and I had started taking Esciptalopram. I felt like I couldn't cope with my fourth different type of medication, 6 weeks weaning myself off the previous ones and then another 6 weeks for the new ones to kick in, I was getting very used to the ups and downs this caused. The reason I changed anti-depressants was because the previous ones were making me incredibly tired, or at least I thought it was that.

It was in September 2010 that I purchased my first car and passed my test first time the following month. I was buzzing though still exhausted. It didn't help that one of my first trips before getting a sat nav was what should have been an hour's drive to IKEA. I went straight from college which was a mistake. I set off around 1pm and didn't get home till 1am. I'd got incredibly lost and must have covered the whole of the North West during those 12 hours. I was pulled over by the police at one point and had to be breathalized, I even got lost after they'd directed me home, it was a nightmare and a trip I've never made since.

The days at college were slightly more bearable knowing I could drive to and from college rather than waiting around on public transport. My car insurance cost £3000, it was crazy but I was too impatient to wait any longer. It also meant that I could sleep in the car on my lunch breaks and get home quicker afterwards for a longer sleep before tea.

By this time I had completely discharged myself from the mental health services as I felt they were no longer benefitting me, I felt more depressed after I'd been than before I went. I considered myself to have pretty much recovered from my depression though I remain on the medication to this day as I have been told there are no side effects for me to keep taking them. I didn't want to change something that was working well.

I started work at a local fast food restaurant for some extra cash though lasted three weeks. The manager was horrible to me and I felt like a second class citizen. I'd also had interviews to work at a funeral directors and as a carer. It was a shame about the funeral directors because the interview went very well, it was the fact I couldn't work 5 days a week that stopped me getting the job. The other interview was a disaster.

 In November 2010 my services were no longer needed as a Painter/Decorator and so got myself a job at a local pub. The first shift was very daunting, it took me a while to get used to where everything was but I managed and came to quite enjoy it. The staff/ boss I worked with were great. It was the first time I had a boss I actually respected and I felt everyone else there were genuine people. I wasn't used to being in those sorts of surroundings and was a little quieter than the rest but everyone was great with me. The job was perfect for me at the time and it helped me to gradually increase my confidence. The shifts were tiring me out but this was a feeling I was used to. A psychiatrist once said to me that "Some people are just born that way" relating to some people being more tired than others. My customer relationship skills weren't the best in the world but my hours gradually increased.

In January of 2011 I decided to go along to a football trial and try out as a goalkeeper. It had been a while since I'd played in a team. As always, my reflex saves were good but I didn't have a clue when to come off my line. The training sessions lasted for 3 hours on a Sunday morning. At the start of the year, it was a new year's resolution to attend church weekly. I felt it was a good thing to do and I wanted to explore the

Bible. I'd also had links with a particular church since I was a toddler but spent the majority of my teenage years rebelling against it. I was attending the evening services at church after playing football for three hours earlier on. After a few weeks it became apparent that I was doing too much and needed some chill time. After all, Sunday is the day of rest.

I had a decision to make. Do I go with my head (football) or my heart (church)? I decided to go with my heart.

I began to enjoy attending church after spending my teen years cursing the very same place. Not only were the sermons interesting but the welcome I received was very warm. Despite not attending for a few years, people remembered me, remembered what I was studying at college, and in general just showed a general interest in how I was. I'd never felt so appreciated before.

It was in February that I decided I wanted to explore deeper. I pulled aside one of the church pastors after an evening service and asked them questions about sin. I truly believed that my sinful thoughts meant I couldn't be a Christian. It was when I realized that these thoughts were completely normal that I really wanted to learn. That same evening, a friend at the church who had always kept in touch when I wasn't attending told me that they could give me an overview of the Bible in less than an hour. I didn't believe them so I took them up on the offer. I met up with this friend the following week and as they had said, gave me an overview of the Bible. I was impressed and at that same meet up felt in my heart that I was a Christian and wanted to be baptized. I realized that I didn't need to know the Bible word for word to be a Christian. I continued to meet up with this friend weekly for the months leading up to my baptism. I felt honored that a highly qualified person would want to meet up with me and teach me parts of the Bible every week.

I then started to meet up weekly with another pastor at the church who took me through a few courses before I made up my mind about being baptized. These courses strengthened my faith and it was then that I'd start thinking about when to be baptized. I then wrote my testimony. I wanted to make sure that it wasn't during the summer time as a lot of my friends/acquaintances would be on holiday. It was on September 11th 2011 that I was baptized. The buzz I got from reading my testimony was incredible. I overcame a fear of reading in public and it also felt incredible that everyone was listening to me. So many times previously, I felt no-one was ever listening to me.

Here is my testimony:

Before I became a Christian

I was born and raised in Southport, my mum is a member of the church here and my dad comes from a Roman Catholic background. I've been coming to church on-and-off since I was a toddler, and am now aged 20.

*I am currently in my third year of university at Edge Hill.
During my childhood, I was diagnosed with what is called Asperger syndrome which basically affects the way in which a person understands other people, talks with other people, and acts with other people.*

This restricted me greatly in my childhood and was the cause of a lot of bullying that went on.

I don't actually remember much that went on in my childhood as it seems a blur apart from the fact I didn't have many friends and home-life was difficult.

I was diagnosed with depression when I was 16 which overtime became more severe, and a few months later I attempted to take my life. I thought I was worthless, hated and not as good as anybody else. For a while after that, my lifestyle consisted of staying in bed all day, with crisis teams coming out to keep an eye on me. Around that time, I was also involved with crime and drugs.

Becoming a Christian

I always believed in my head I was a Christian in the way I acted and always told people I was a Christian. I didn't drink much alcohol, and had high morals – these were always the cause of relationship break-ups.

I tried to live the life of a Christian but always had doubt in my heart about God's existence.

However, it was after an evening service at church earlier on this year that I spoke to Pastor A about sin. It was when he said that everyone struggles with sin that I realized I didn't have to be perfect to become a Christian. As Christians we can find ourselves in situations presently where we need to rely on God to deal with whatever comes at us.
Before becoming a Christian, there was something that stopped me

making the commitment earlier, but I then realised after some research that there were Christians in similar situations.

I also spoke to Person M that night who said he would give me an overview on the Bible, it was after the overview that I became a Christian.

After that I understood more the true meaning of the Bible and I started to pray daily.

Person M has been highly influential ever since and has increased my understanding of what it means to be a Christian by explaining what each story means and the importance of them.

Pastor S has also been very influential and both have helped me a great deal in the early stages of my Christian life.

How God has worked

Looking back, I believe at the time I was in hospital (January 2008) following the overdose, that God had given me the golden opportunity to come to him – which I didn't see at the time.

There have been times since I have become a Christian that I have considered taking my life, the difference between now and before is that I know God can pull me through.

I believe God has put me through all he did because he saw I was struggling and needed help; I believe he has made me into a stronger person. With God, he has given me the belief that I can successfully achieve things He has planned for me without giving up. I now have the determination to be successful in God's eyes.

I also hope I can be of help, particularly to those who can relate to my story, that God has worked and changed my life around and that he can do so to anyone.

Song

The song that you will hear shortly is called 'The Prayer' by a man called Rhydian Roberts, who is a big inspiration to me. He is an active Christian and the song means a lot to me when he sings it.

I then became a member of the church at the Lord's Supper the following month. It felt great having a church family. I'd never felt like I'd had a proper family before.

Due to ill health, I'm not always able to make it to church yet everyone remains supportive.

Chapter 3: Leading up to an M.E. Diagnosis

In the summer of 2011 I had completed my foundation degree and decided to stay on for the extra year to complete my honors degree. This year would be spent at a university. It was a 20 minute drive from me which suited me down to the ground.

It was very hard making friends as the majority of my classmates over the past couple of years had picked different subjects to me. I was the newbie and university life didn't appeal to me. I wasn't a regular drinker and usually went on nights out to fit in rather than because I wanted to. I turned up for the majority of the lectures and left straight after. I didn't make any friends; I was constantly tired and didn't have the energy. I was a loner and found the year very difficult.

It was a shame really because the university itself was great and there were many things I never got to experience. I wasn't in the right state of mind for it looking back but I managed. I wanted to get my education out of the way as quick as possible.

It was in June 2012 that I graduated from University. I graduated with a 2:2 Honors Degree in Business & Management. Not a great result but under the circumstances was relatively satisfactory. I didn't attend the graduation as I didn't enjoy my time there and was just relieved to get my degree. I very quickly started to look at business related jobs. It was within 2 weeks of the graduation that I got a new job. It turned out the job description was very misleading. Persuading small businesses to change their phone package and being told not to leak certain information didn't sit well with me. The money was potentially great but that didn't stop me from leaving after a week. They were long days; I was getting up at 7am and arriving home at 8pm. Every train ride home I felt exhausted, but despite pains in my legs and complete cognitive exhaustion,

I didn't think much of it.

July had arrived and I was wondering what my next step would be. I came to realize that a lot of business related jobs involved long hours and knew my body would have difficulty coping with that. I thought I was just "one of those people" who gets tired more easily than others. One afternoon, I was thinking about what I really wanted to do regardless of earnings and qualifications etc. I thought "what am I passionate about?" Football (didn't start out young enough), Wrestling (it requires a lot of training and no guarantee of work), Music (I had no previous experience at this point) and the list went on.

These were all unrealistic options until I thought of one thing, fitness. I'd always been a regular face at the gym, knowledgeable about weight training in particular and it was something I'd enjoy teaching. That same afternoon I searched online for Personal Training and at the top of the search results appeared the Personal Training Academy I ended up going to. I had a phone conversation the next day. 6 weeks seemed such a short space of time to be qualified as not only a level 3 Personal Trainer, but also qualified to teach gym based-boxing, studio cycling and circuit training as well as gaining a certificate in sports nutrition. I was always a good saver so delved into my savings account and paid the fee upfront. It was a lot but I was confident it would be worth it. I was excited that I'd finally found something I felt confident doing.

That summer was pretty good as far as I can remember. I met up with a friend usually once a week a fair distance from me whilst seeing my other friends the other days. The friend I met up with once a week had Myalgic Encephalomyelitis though at that time had no idea what it was. I grew quite close to this friend and they started to tell me more about the illness. It seriously made me wonder whether I had something similar. I began to tell them what symptoms I was experiencing: pains in my legs, fatigue, concentration difficulties amongst others. The symptoms were similar to my friends though mine were fairly mild at that point. I then began researching more about the illness and decided to book myself an appointment with my GP. It was around August time that I saw my GP and told them about the symptoms I was experiencing. I'd previously seen my GP several times before about fatigue before but nothing ever came of it. I told them about Myalgic Encephalomyelitis and they admitted their knowledge of the illness was limited. They did however have a contact address at a hospital near to me who specialized in the illness. The same day, my GP put in a referral for me to see a chronic fatigue specialist. They said I should hear within 6 weeks. I always knew there was something wrong but didn't quite know what, I finally felt like I was getting somewhere.

A few months prior to this, I'd started taking Ice Skating lessons. It was always something I wanted to do. I started attending lessons at an Olympic Stadium not far from where I lived. Well, it was an hour's drive there and an hour's drive back, the lessons were only 30 minutes and it was on a Saturday morning. I had to leave the house by 8am having only got in from work around 1am the same morning, followed by another long shift that evening. It was very tiring but I really wanted to stick at it. I was always steady on my legs, never fell over but I noticed that something wasn't quite right. My legs felt a lot heavier and my body overall just wasn't responding the same way I was used to, I just put it down to lack of practice but it was like my overall balance had deteriorated.

I very suddenly had a thought. "If I really do have Myalgic Encephalomyelitis then how on earth am I going to get through a very intense 6 week Personal Training course?! Will it make me worse?" Whilst researching about the illness, it became apparent to me that over-exertion made symptoms worse. I'd already parted with half of my entire savings so had to go through with it. The rest of that summer was spent worrying about how this course was going to go.

September had arrived and I was about to start the course. Up at 6:30am for 2 10 minute drives to and from the train station, and 2, 2 hour long plus train journeys. That's not forgetting the 10 minute walk to and from the train station from the gym I was attending, plus a very intense day of learning. The academy was located in a studio room at the gym. To say I was exhausted after the 1st day was an understatement, the cognitive difficulties I was having meant not that much was going in. I was very knowledgeable about this sort of thing but my mental exhaustion was starting to really have an effect on me.

At one time I would have reveled in the practical side of things but not this time. I had to lie down for an hour every day before having something to eat in the evening just to muster up some energy to see through the night. After a few days of crushing my brain mentally, the class was practicing on the different bits of gym equipment to prepare for the exams. The exams consisted of multiple choice questions and also a practical assessment. I remember starting up the treadmill and doing a gentle jog. After about 30 seconds the muscles in my legs began to tighten and ache. I thought I could maybe run it off but after 3 minutes I found it hard to walk. My legs were like jelly; I was more upset than anything because I used to do lots of running and always kept in athletic shape. Not only that, I began to get paranoid that other members of the class were thinking I was lazy as I began to do as little as I could physically. I don't think my tutors really knew what M.E. was but then why should they? I had never even heard of the illness a couple of months back. I knew a fair bit about the technical side of things when it came to fitness though learning about the bodies different systems was new for me. I remember one the tutors saying that it took them 4 years at college to get all the qualifications that were involved in this course, which just shows how intense it really was. I got my level 2 in Fitness instructing after just 3 weeks, a qualification that would take a year to get at most colleges. I was really praying that I was going to hear about this referral. I was praying over 10 times a day about other issues and my mind was all over the place. I managed to continue the course and totally dismissed my original plan of staying behind after the day for an hour's workout; it was just too much for me. We spent odd days practicing boxing/circuit training and studio cycling. Studio cycling is also known as spinning, an indoor cycling workout that typically lasts between 45 minutes to an hour. My legs couldn't take the spinning and I came to dread it, not only that but my feet were too big for the pedals. Amongst all this we were studying the practical and theory side of Personal Training which is more advanced than Fitness Instructing. The mental exhaustion was unbearable. Not only that but every day my legs were bothering me, they would ache non-stop. The sensation became normal for me and I just put up with it hoping it would go. I just about struggled through the practical assessment but the mental exhaustion I was experiencing meant it took me several goes to pass my level 3 theory exam.

I was just relieved to have completed the course in one piece despite the effect it had had on my body. Or at least I thought I was... I wasn't going to get any rest at all. Towards the end of the course I had foolishly agreed to go to an interview about starting up as a Personal Trainer at a gym near to me. I was still working part-time at the pub too. I thought the opportunity was too good to miss. I wanted to build a client base at a local gym before moving on to home visits. It wasn't as simple as that, I hadn't done my research properly. I later found out I had to attend a business course in London for 2 days, somewhere I'd never been before and somewhere far away from my little town, Southport. My body was telling me not to do it but my head was telling me to go for it and so I went with my head. I ended up having to be driven for over half an hour to the train station followed by a 2 hour plus train journey. I was up and ready before 5am and shattered before I had even set off. I remember for those two days living off McDonald's. Stuff the healthy diet; I'm sticking to what I know. I stayed at a Travel Lodge and was in bed before 7pm that evening. Most evenings I wouldn't even have had my tea by that point. To say the course was a money-making con is an understatement. After paying £3000 to get my qualifications, I found myself another £300 plus down due to the course. Maybe it was good information but my mind could not cope. I was determined to make it work. The train journey home from London was agonizing. I remember clutching onto the seats as I was hobbling along to the toilet because I could barely walk. Didn't look great with "Personal Trainer" written on my back though. I arrived home around 10pm and started my new job the following day. I started my new job tomorrow... Luckily I was able to arrive mid-afternoon but still, I was getting very little rest. Everyone was pleasant when I arrived but it was a very small gym over crowded with Personal Trainers on the lead up to Christmas, it was tough. I managed to book a few sessions in and lead some small classes for members as well as doing a few inductions. I knew from research that

January was the month to be picking up lots of clients. Lots have a New Year's Resolution to join a gym, previous statistics showed that. Experiences of other trainers showed that. 3 weeks had gone and things were going Ok, not brilliantly but it was promising.

I was about to take my first spinning class the following Monday which I was buzzing about. I'd sorted out all the songs and had a particular routine planned. However, the Sunday night before I was at church operating the sound desk. The pains in my legs became unbearable, to the point I was thinking about leaving before the end of the service. They'd never been this bad before. As soon as the service ended I drove myself up to the hospital, I was in the waiting room for a few hours in agony. I had to lie down on the seats in the waiting room because I was in that much agony. I was struggling to walk and was seriously worried as to whether I could drive back or not. There was still no sign of a referral. The doctor I saw knew very little about M.E. so not a lot could be done. I asked if there was anything they could give me to help me get around when I was struggling; the doctor said that they couldn't do anything as there were no visibly broken bones. I was prescribed strong painkillers which had little effect.

I went to the doctors around 3 days later. I was losing a lot of blood and had to be taken to hospital ASAP. A friend had to take my car home as I wasn't able to. I had a nasty bout of Gastroenteritis. It was the worst sort of virus I'd ever experienced, it was incredibly painful and I lost so much weight. Within in the space of a few weeks I'd lost around a stone in weight. Luckily, I had to stay overnight... maybe 2 but I honestly can't remember. However, it took me a while till I stopped passing blood as frequently.

Another 3 days had passed and I found myself in Exeter. I'd promised beforehand a while back that I'd go with my dad to see my half sister who I'd never met before. I felt ill but didn't like letting people down. It was only an overnight stay and I didn't have to drive so it wasn't too bad and I managed to get plenty of rest.

When I got home I started to do more extensive research on M.E. and began to realize how unhelpful doctors could be. I spoke to lots of people with the illness and was asking for advice. I decided to take the 1st move and invest in some crutches. They were great. They didn't entirely ease the pain but they helped, I felt more secure and able to get about that little bit more easily. The problem was how could I explain this to my friends, family, work-colleagues? At this point, I had cut my hours down at the pub to just 1 evening; I needed some source of income and worked through the pain. I was getting more orders wrong and had to sit down round the back when it was quiet. I decided to keep the referral quiet until anything had come of it. It was crazy, using crutches throughout the week and standing behind a bar at weekend. How does that work? Well that's M.E. for you. The Saturday evening shifts were having a negative effect on my Sunday's. I was struggling to make it to church and spent the entire days resting. How could I explain this to my boss, and my friends for that matter? I went in to collect something from the pub one day with my crutches, how could I explain that? It felt embarrassing; I wouldn't have blamed my boss and the rest of the staff if they didn't believe me at all. To them it was a very quick change but for me it had been a build up over a number of months that I had kept quiet about. It was strange to say for least, even for me.

Chapter 4: My First Year with M.E.

I received a slip through my door saying I had to collect an item; I didn't have a clue what it was. I wasn't allowed to pick it up the same day so went the next morning. I had to pay to receive a letter from the hospital. The funny thing was that there were 3 people in the house the previous day and no-one had heard the door go. I opened the letter and it and it was a date to see a consultant at the hospital, fantastic... well it would have been if the date of the appointment hadn't been a day before I received the letter, not the day the slip was posted through my door but the day before that. I was fuming. I had to wait a few more weeks before the appointment was rearranged. 10th of January 2013, I remember that day very well.

The date had come and I was nervous but hopeful, I just wanted an answer. I was in 2 minds, 1 was hoping that I didn't have

M.E. and the other was hoping I did just so I could get an answer as to why I was feeling like I did. The consultant was excellent, this is what they wrote:

> *Typed 6th Feb 2013:*
> *Follow up: Chronic fatigue specialist services*
> *Diagnosis: Chronic fatigue syndrome (Oxford CDC criteria 12 month history probable relapse)*
> *Depression (stable five years)*
> *Asperger's spectrum disease – diagnosed aged nine no medical input*
> *Many thanks for referring this very pleasant 21 year old gentleman who attended clinic today. He provides a complex history and was thus reviewed at the diagnostic clinic. His history is summarized below.*
> *He has complained of an ongoing fluctuating fatigue for 12 months which has worsened and of insidious onset. In retrospect there have probably been previous episodes of fluctuating fatigue in the past. He describes sleeping during the day time and a poor and unrefreshed*

sleep pattern. Alongside these symptoms he possibly describes exercise payback as well as reduced concentration and short term memory in keeping with brain fogging. There are also symptoms of myalgia with leg pain, he was seen two months ago in hospital out patients and treated with some Naproxen with no real clinical improvement. However, the concern was of exclusion criteria pertaining to chronic fatigue syndrome and I discussed this with him at the end of the appointment in some depth.

The first concern was of the Asperger's spectrum, however, this was diagnosed at aged nine, from the description sounds mild in nature, there was no medical intervention and he has subsequently been discharged. Similarly he does have a background history of low mood and depression. He was managed in the community but never received any form of behavioral psychotherapy and this is currently stable. His systems review is otherwise unremarkable.

His medication is as above, he suffers no allergies. He lives with his mother and one brother, occasionally smokes and drinks little alcohol. He was previously employed but is currently not working and denies any illicit drug use.

He tells me he hadn't previously been examined and today on examination he wasn't clubbed, cyanosed, jaundice or anemic, there was no lymphadenopathy. His pulse was 70 beats per minute regularly regular. Blood pressure was 120/70 lying and standing in both arms. Both heart sounds were heard with nil added. His JVP wasn't raised, his chest was clear and his abdomen was soft. Despite the background history of low mood I am content that the symptoms of fluctuating fatigue are separate to these and that he is suffering from chronic fatigue syndrome according to both Oxford and CDC criteria. I have provided information relating to aetiology, pathophysiology and are management plan and felt that Mr Evans would benefit from entering

> *into the treatment programme. I also explained to him that unfortunately one aspect which he would significantly benefit from (our clinical psychology service) has currently been suspended while we wait for new appointments. However, he should in the mean time attend the rest of the programme and I have made the appropriate referrals. If you have any queries please do not hesitate to contact me.*

I had mixed feelings about this result but overall I was just happy that I had finally gotten an answer. I left the pub around the same time as with the official diagnosis, I knew it wasn't sustainable for me. This was the first time in my life I hadn't been studying or hadn't been working; I hadn't done my research properly and was expecting to be able to get back into Personal Training by that summer. How wrong was I? I'd spoken to the owner of another gym just out of town who was keen to give me a go but circumstances made this impossible. I didn't want to be making my health worse and I didn't feel it was right having clients when my health was far from 100%.

I was at the age where I felt my career would really set off; I'd always had a very businesslike mind. Falling ill meant my ambitions had to be put on hold. I felt like I was at a big stand still and it was very hard trying to adjust my lifestyle.

Despite warnings and concerns, I decided to foolishly carry on going to the gym. I thought that if I halve my workouts, use a slightly lower weight and sat down on the machines whilst resting in between sets that I could keep it up. I was exhausting myself so much that a half hour workout would wipe me out for the whole day and part of the day after. I wanted to bulk up as I'd lost a lot of weight over the past few months due to ill health. I was barely weighing in at over 13 stone when at my heaviest was close to 15 stone. At 6ft 3, I carry the weight well. I was a fitness fanatic who couldn't accept that the wise thing was to take a break from it all.

I was working out in the morning and hobbling around on crutches in the afternoon and it became increasingly more difficult for me to keep up what I was doing. I decided to cancel my gym membership and just stick to a healthy diet. This lasted a few weeks. My mind then became focused on setting up a weights bench in the shed which I did. I had the equipment from previous years and decided to use it. I thought that if I could work out without leaving the house then I could keep it up. This didn't last long and I began working out less and less. I now do a lot more spaced out and less intense exercise but it has taken me a while to find something my body can cope with, it's far from what I want but then this was all about adjusting my lifestyle.

Around this time, I had been contacted about a "cure" for M.E. and was persuaded into a phone call. I knew it would be nonsense, if there was a cure for M.E. then surely doctors would know about it. I was intrigued to hear about this. It turns out that it was just a few very over priced items that "may" relieve a few symptoms if you're lucky. They said I'd be cured in 6 weeks... One of those items was Aloe Vera. We never spoke again.

Social media was and still is great for connecting with other people in a similar position to me but it bothered me greatly that I had no-one locally who I felt really understood me. There was one person from the church who I met up with occasionally who'd been through the same therapy program that I was going to be partaking in. It was helpful sharing experiences but I still felt isolated. I knew a fair few people through social media who had M.E. but not one of them was a guy in their twenties.

I tried talking to my friends about my problems but this was mostly welcomed with an awkward silence. There were odd comments being made that I wasn't happy with and I began to feel more trapped. My mum understood me best though I still had my doubts. My best friend told me that if they wanted to know more about the illness then they would look it up in their own time. They felt like I was forcing them to understand. I later got an apology but it really hurt me. Since then I have very rarely mentioned anything to do with M.E. It makes answering simple questions such as "How are you?" a lot more awkward. I started to feel a lot more isolated and soon came to realize that this was very normal for a lot of M.E. sufferers. I pushed myself to do things but I was starting to worry that I was doing too much. Afternoon naps had been the norm for a while now.

I had a medical coming up for my ESA in May which I was dreading; I had heard how unfair they were and didn't have very high hopes. I didn't want to be seen as a benefits scrounger but I was unable to work. I had a genuine and thorough diagnosis yet people still didn't understand.

My cognitive function was deteriorating; my mum had to help me fill out the forms. She had to become my appointee and I felt like a kid. How else could I fill these endless forms out? I got headaches from very short conversations. However, I knew I was lucky to have an appointee.

The following form was filled out in on the 27th March 2013:

> ***Tell us about any help you would need if you have to go for a face-to-face assessment.***
> *Find stairs difficult but will have someone with me to assist me. Would prefer a local appointment as find driving long distances difficult.*
> ***Please use the space on this page to tell us:***
> ***What your illness, disability or condition is***
> ***How it affects you, and***
> ***When it started***
> ***If your condition varies over time, tell us how.***
> ***Please tell us about any aids you use, such as a wheelchair or hearing aid***
> ***Anything else you think we should know about your illness or disabilities.***

I suffer from Chronic Fatigue Syndrome. This means I have a severe lack of energy and feel constantly drained. I have unrefreshing sleep. I also suffer from short-term memory loss. My muscles feel tight and are often painful which means my mobility is severely affected. My symptoms started gradually but started to increase a lot about a year ago. I visited my GP throughout this time. My symptoms have been a lot more severe for the past 6 months. Some days are worse than others, on a bad day I am unable to cope with anything. Even on better days I struggle getting around, and often can't leave the house. I find the condition very debilitating. I have also suffered from depression for over 5 years and take medication for this. I also have Aspergers Syndrome – I was diagnosed when I was 9 years old. I also suffer from Irlen Syndrome and this means I have to wear tinted glasses.

Tell us about all your hospital and clinic visits here

I am waiting to start a treatment programme at hospital. I should hear about this any time now.

How far can you move safely and repeatedly on level ground without needing to stop?

On a bad day, I would probably have to stop maybe every 100 metres as I suffer from severe tiredness. I often feel light-headed and have to sit down. The more I move the muscular pain and tightness gets worse in my legs. I also get out of breath very easily and quickly. I use crutches to get around. I have to move very slowly.

How long can you stay in one place, either standing, sitting, or a combination of the two, without help from another person, without pain or exhaustion?

I can't stand for a length of time because the muscular pain increases the longer I stand for. When I then sit down, I feel instantly drained and often light-headed. I would need to lie down in less time than 30 minutes.

Can you communicate a simple message to other people such as the presence of something dangerous?

My Aspergers affects my communication abilities. I find it very difficult to express myself and find it hard to understand others sometimes.

Can you understand simple messages from other people by reading large size print or using Braille?

My hearing is fine. My problems are in understanding what people mean, and in following a conversation. My concentration problems do not help with this.

Can you get around a place that you haven't been to before without help?

I tend to get lost easily as I have no sense of direction. I also have Irlen Syndrome and have to wear tinted spectacles.

While you are awake, how often do you faint or have fits or blackouts?

I don't lose consciousness but can feel very dazed and disorientated at times.

Can you learn how to do a more complicated task such as using as washing machine?

Barry's inability to concentrate makes it very difficult for him to take information and instructions in. He finds it hard to follow a logical order of doing things due to his Aspergers and Chronic Fatigue has made things much worse.

Can you manage to plan, start and finish daily tasks?

Barry needs constant support and encouragement to accomplish the most basic daily tasks. He finds it extremely hard to get up due to always having unrefreshed sleep. He is as tired as when he went to bed. His memory is very bad and he needs constant reminders of what he needs to do next. His lack of concentration makes it almost impossible for him to follow tasks through.

Can you cope with small changes

to your routine if they are unexpected?

Barry's Aspergers means he likes to stick to routines. He dislikes any unexpected changes and gets very stressed. His chronic fatigue can interfere with 'normal' routines which he finds very hard to cope with. He gets frustrated, upset and extremely stressed.

Can you meet people you don't know without feeling too anxious or scared?

Barry finds it hard meeting people he doesn't know. He finds it difficult concentrating and understanding strangers and making himself understood. At appointments, I have to go with him so he can understand what is being said to him. Also to help him say what he wants to say himself. Otherwise he will forget things or not understand information given to him. He feels very uncomfortable with people he is not familiar with.

How often do you behave in a way

> **which upsets other people?**
> *I get very frustrated due to my limitations. I find it very stressful being unable to concentrate for any length of time. I know this makes me difficult to live with. I upset people as I can appear aggressive due to my frustrations.*
>
> *I have filled this in as Barry's Appointee (I am his mum). We both went through all the questions altogether. If you require any further information please don't hesitate to contact me.*

I felt like a baby having someone to help me fill out a form but that's what was needed. I was having cognitive problems so needed the help. I felt the line of questioning was inappropriate for someone who suffered with M.E. so what was the medical going to be like? It felt like I was being questioned about my Aspergers rather than my M.E. which wasn't why I was attending the medical even though my M.E. symptoms had significantly worsened some of the Aspergers symptoms.

It was time for the medical and I wasn't looking forward. The person I saw was pleasant enough but as I suspected, the medical was completely inappropriate for someone with my illness. I was asked very little about my M.E. and was asked to do things like raise my hands and legs without assistance. This wasn't the problem; the problem was the muscle pain, the cognitive difficulties, the extreme fatigue, the muscle weakness and most of all, the post-exertional malaise. They weren't going to see how the medical affected me. I spent the rest of that week housebound and a lot of that time lying down.

Over a month later, I had the result and to no surprise I was deemed fit to work. Here's what the letter said:

> *WCA Disallowance*
>
> *I have superseded the decision of the Decision Maker awarding Employment and Support Allowance from and including 10 Feb 2013 following a*

medical assessment.

The Limited Capability for Work Assessment test of incapacity assesses the ability to perform specific physical activities and, where there is a mental illness, to cope with day to day living. Points are awarded to reflect limitations and a score of 15 points is needed to satisfy the test. The assessment cannot take account of the requirement of a person's normal occupation.

Mr Barry John Evans completed a questionnaire in which he identified difficulties in relation to his Visual Problem, Chronic Fatigue Syndrome and Mental Health Problem. Mr Evans was examined by a Healthcare Professional (HCP) on 08 May 2013 when his functional capability was assessed.

In his questionnaire Mr Evans described difficulties with mobilising, standing & sitting, getting around safely, communicating with people, other people communicating with you, learning how to do tasks, initiating actions, coping with change, coping with social situations and behaving appropriately with other people.

Mobilising and standing & sitting
Mr Evans used crutches to the assessment; he caught the train and walked in a timely manner about 400 metres from the train station to the MEC.

In the lower limb assessment the HCP found no abnormalities – Mr Evans had good power and there was no evidence of muscle wastage.

The HCP observed Mr Evans sit for 40 minutes, rise twice without physical assistance from another person, stand independently for 2 minutes without difficulty, use two crutches to walk 12 metres to the examination room, get onto the couch without assistance and appear to have no difficulty using a step to get onto the couch.

In his typical day history Mr Evans stated he has problems washing and dressing himself, he will go downstairs a step at a time, avoids these if possible, so spends a lot of time upstairs, he makes breakfast and then does only basic things such as gets himself a big bottle of water. He stated he tries to get himself out the house daily and he goes to a coffee shop everyday and drives there which is about 4 minutes away – he drives a manual car and stated he drives locally only (5-10 minutes max) and avoids driving out of Southport. He stated he rarely goes to the shops/supermarket and he will take his mother to the supermarket and then sits in the car as feels going in will affect him for the next day and he can sit and use a computer for hours.

The evidence indicates Mr Evans would have no significant problems with mobilising 200m or remaining at a work station, either standing or sitting or a combination of both for more than an hour. I have therefore not awarded any points for these descriptors.

Getting around safely, communicating with people and other people communicating

In the assessment Mr Evans stated he

had no speech or hearing problems. The HCP found Mr Evans visual acuity was 6/6 using both eyes without correction and using both eyes she was able to read N8 print on a reading test type chart from a distance of 35cm without correction. The HCP observed Mr Evans had no difficulty negotiating doorways and furniture within the examination centre.

In his typical day Mr Evans stated he has problems visual problems reading black writing on white paper and often has sensitivity to light and uses tinted glasses to correct this (he did not take his tinted glasses to the assessment), he stated he will try to read but finds his brain fog limits this and he is able to use a computer to play games and use the internet and he will spend hours on this.

The evidence indicates Mr Evans would have no significant problems with navigation, making himself understood or understanding communication. I have therefore not awarded any points for these descriptors.

Mental, cognitive and intellectual function

In the mental health assessment the HCP found Mr Evans' mental state examination was unremarkable. The HCP observed Mr Evans' movements were slow and his mood was labile and he spoke well, appeared to have good rapport and coped well at interview.

In his typical day history Mr Evans is able to self care, he stated he wanted to learn how to play the piano keyboard and was awaiting arrival of one and he spends hours on his computer playing games and on the internet. Mr Evans stated he tries to get himself out of the house daily, he can go to his GP surgery alone, he can drive a manual care locally for 5-10 minutes, he sees his father couple of times a week who will pick him up and he goes for coffee or to his flat and he has a friend who visits every week. Mr Evans stated he feels uncomfortable on the phone but is able to do this and he has 2 dogs, 2 cats, 3 rabbits, 2 guinea pigs, a gerbil, 3 rats and 2 birds and stated his mother keeps these clean. The evidence indicates Mr Evans would have no significant problems with learning how to do tasks, initiating actions, coping with change, coping with social situations and behaving appropriately with other people. I have therefore not awarded any points for these descriptors. I am satisfied that the descriptors have been fully justified with clinical findings, observations and extracts taken from the typical day history provided by Mr Evans. The medical report of 08 May 2013 was appropriate, complete and covered all the area of incapacity described by Mr Evans as well as including a comprehensive typical day history and full set of clinical findings.

6. *In his appeal Mr Evans has stated that the questions asked in the Work Capability Assessment were not appropriate for someone with his condition. Mr Evans has provided a detailed outline of how his condition*

> *affects him under the activities and descriptors used at the Work Capability Assessment.*

This result didn't surprise me although I wasn't very happy about some of the things that were said. First of all, I was referred to as a "she" in one part, fair enough as people make typing errors from time to time. However, it was stated several times that I sat for hours at my computer which I never said. I said I left my computer on for hours but in no way did I say I used it for hours. They were very good at twisting my words and putting words into my mouth without me realizing. Another niggle was the fact it was stated that I went out for coffees every day. First of all, I don't think my body could take coffee every day and second of all, I only left the house a few times a week and that was if I was lucky. I said that I'd try to get some fresh air daily by sitting outside in the back yard but in no way did I say that I went out daily for coffees. I was also a little confused as to why my slow movements were mentioned under the mental/ cognitive and intellectual function section? Maybe my slow movements were due to the fact that I was using crutches and find it a lot more difficult to walk than I used to due to muscle pain and fatigue. There was also very little mention of my M.E. symptoms like the pain and also the after effects. I also felt it was inappropriate to mention the animals I lived with seeing as I did very little to contribute to the looking after of them.

I was starting to panic and my stress levels were raising. What if I had to go to job interviews? I can't see employers' wanting to take on someone who had the problems I was having. It was a ridiculous situation and not something I could talk about to others. I felt ashamed about the whole thing and felt like others were looking at me thinking I was a fraud. It wasn't a nice feeling but what else could I do? It's not my fault I have an invisible illness that so many tend to completely disregard.

The decision was appealed against. A series of phone calls were kept on record around this time. I found it hard making phone calls so had help with these also. These were the notes that were kept:

> *27/5/13 – eligibility was turned down due to not passing medical. Told could appeal or sign on for employment. Sending us an appeal form today.*
> *6/6/13 – rang day received letter about claim for employment and support allowance. No record of it having been sent. Result of last appeal was no entitlement. We should have been notified but were not. Asked re medical – passed to decision maker on 17/5/13. No result yet. Ring again in a week.*
> *8/7/13 - Saw doctor. They said GP's have been told they cannot write any letters etc of support. They can answer queries if they write to them.*
> *8/7/13 - Rang ESA to check if received. Hadn't and said to ring wed 10/7. Told to get another sick note from doctor as present one is invalid from medical result. Make another appointment with GP.*

11/7/13 – Rang – they confirmed appeal was received on Monday 8/7/13. Informed me I was given incorrect info last phone call. Med certificate is still valid – or else payment due tomorrow wouldn't have gone through. They need another certificate by 9th August. Payments will carry on until appeal is settled.
17/7/13 – They rang whilst I was at work (mum). Said would ring back at 4pm. I rang them as will be out. Said no record of who rang – will mark my file and say to ring me sometime tomorrow.

Got me on mobile, arranged they will contact me on 22/7/13 about 10.30am to go through appeal form.
22/7/13 – Went through appeal form. They will contact doctor for support. We probably won't hear until late August regards the result of appeal. Read letter dated 22/7/13. Not changed their decision. Being passed to independent appeal tribunal.

It would be months before I heard about the tribunal date.

It was June and Cognitive Behavioral Therapy was coming up. There was a group session held at the hospital on the 12th June. I felt it was quite Ironic that the room was based in the psychology department though due to lack of funding, the department was placed wherever was convenient. Unfortunately, I was late to the session as I assumed there would be a toilet on the same floor as the room the session I was in. I was wrong.

I felt the session was aimed at sufferers who knew very little about the illness. I thought the majority of the information given was good though I learned nothing new. One thing I took from the session was a visual demonstration shown using jugs of water, orange juice and cups. The aim of the demonstration was to show us how to use our energy wisely with the water representing our energy. There were a fair number of us, probably around 30 but half of those were partners/relatives. Apart from a sufferers husband and my own father who drove me down, I was the only guy in the whole room. The ratio was women to men was incredible, if I said that for every 9 women I knew with M.E. there was 1 male then I might be overestimating. I was given an information pack at the end of the session, too much information for an M.E. sufferer to be reading through. Pages and pages of words that to be honest was mostly common sense. Things like tips on how to get a good sleep and what to do when you feel your symptoms worsening.

Here's what the letter said:

> *Dear patient*
> *Thank you for attending the CFS group information session. We hope that you found it useful.*
> *We would be grateful if you could complete the evaluation form and return it in the envelope provided. Your feedback will help the team to consider what works well and what can be improved.*
> *Now spend time familiarising yourself with the starter pack. Then you can start to implement strategies to manage your condition.*
> *You may decide you have enough*

information now to see your condition improve, without further sessions or that our approaches do not suit your needs.

However, after you have made some changes you may decide that you would like further help, support or advice.

If you would like to meet one of the therapy team to discuss how you have used the information in the starter pack, please complete and return the slip in the envelope provided.

You will be seen as soon as possible but may have to wait some time, due to service demands and staffing levels, so it is important that you continue to use the advice provided. If you do not return this slip within the next 6 weeks we will assume that you have decided that you do not wish to be seen and you will be discharged back to the care of your GP.

Yours sincerely
The CFS Therapy Team

I wasn't sure that the service would be beneficial to me but I decided to give it a go. After all, you only live once. I'd heard extremely mixed reviews about it. I spoke to several people about it that'd been through the whole thing before. Everyone had one thing in common with what they were saying; they advised me to approach with caution. Research has found that a very high percentage of sufferers have found this sort of therapy has made them worse. There are so many different therapies, processes and techniques which I won't name but one thing strikes me and that is that if you already have a good knowledge of M.E. and how your body works then these different techniques are of little benefit and in many ways are steps backwards.

However, I was very open-minded and took all the advice I could get on board. After all, I was struggling to fully understand my own illness so any advice was welcome though currently I feel I have a pretty good understanding and being a Personal Trainer helps with knowing how the body works.

The next month or so after the session was fairly non-eventful. Lots of rest and regular naps were the highlight. I'd started up a DVD collection as I was so limited and thought that could be something I could do when I need to rest. I got very into my crime dramas but I didn't want to fall into the trap of becoming a T.V. junkie. I wasn't someone who liked to sit down watching Jeremy Kyle each morning, not because I wasn't up in time but because I wanted my time to be spent wisely. I'd planned to do a bit more reading but I was finding it increasingly difficult to read without getting headaches, even when wearing my rose tinted specs. I have a decent book collection but I honestly don't think I could name you a book I have that I've managed to read from start to finish.

It was summer time and I decided to go camping with a few friends. They were keen on the idea and I didn't want to let them down though I knew it would probably do me more harm than good. To be fair, they did ask me if I'd be Ok to go health wise which I greatly appreciated.

The camping trip to Bala in Wales had been booked and I had vastly underestimated the journey. I was the only one who could drive so I couldn't let everyone else down. I said an hour and a half would be the limit but the journey ended up lasting over 2 hours with very little time spent resting at services. Unsurprisingly, I was drained by time I got there. I did little to help set up the tent as I just needed to rest though I felt I couldn't explain this. I pushed myself further than I would have done normally.

The first night was a nightmare, I didn't have a pillow and the floor underneath was hard. To say I was in a bad mood was an understatement. I was tired and needed my beauty sleep. I spent the entire night sleeping in the car wishing I hadn't gone. Things improved the next day as I found an air bed in the village. I was finding it hard to keep up with my friends but pushed myself so I could, to an extent. My crutch became my soul mate.

We stayed for 4 days and the majority of the time was spent resting, the weather was nice and I was grateful we spent the majority of the time near the tent.

On the last day, I waited in the car whilst the others went for a walk as my legs weren't up to it. We'd found a nice pub which did decent food and was devastated the previous day when we had lunch their and the fish supply had run out, not only that but my friend but got final piece. The small portions overall when camping was difficult for me. I had a very big appetite and lost a few pounds over the few days we were there. I needed my food and ate large portions at home. I'm the sort of guy who could order a 20 inch pizza and eat it all then still be hungry. That however, doesn't happen often as I follow a very healthy diet.

Anyway, back to the camping. I felt exhausted even before the journey back home so wasn't looking forward to it. I managed it but my symptoms had gotten a lot worse. I had bad pains and felt very weak but kept quiet about it. I was so relieved to be home, I had a nice warm bed to get into and a nice big meal to eat. The animals were always excited to see me too.

I spent the most part of the next week in bed. I spent more time in it than I did out of it. Was it worth it? To be honest, probably not. I felt terrible but again, kept quiet about it.

This was the highlight of my summer and I did very little else. I wanted to be out in the sun more but my body was too fatigued. I previously relished staying out in the sun but the heat was just too draining for me. Ironic seeing as my body temperature is cold a lot of the time but that's the way it was. I could quite easily go out on a hot day wearing a leather jacket and a pair of gloves yet sometimes on a cooler day I could feel better in just a t-shirt. It made it somewhat difficult knowing what to wear when leaving the house, though by this point I wasn't leaving the house much anyway.

September had arrived and I made an incredibly foolish decision. Me and my friend booked a holiday to Portugal. It was very spur of the moment but I fancied the idea of relaxing in the sun whilst getting away from reality for a bit. I felt it would do me good but I never gave it much thought, I seemed to totally disregard things like flying and waiting at the airport.

We arrived at the airport around an hour before our flight was due, but somehow we nearly missed the flight. I'd never eaten a fast food meal so quick, it was around 3 minutes. I couldn't fly off without eating, I was starving. Half running to catch a plane with a walking stick and luggage isn't a very fond memory of mine. It was no surprise that the pains had worsened after that.

We arrived and had a transfer by shuttle. They dropped us off at the wrong hotel and I was fuming, I did think that the hotel we arrived at looked a lot nicer than the one we had booked though. I was drained and was ready for bed.

The first night was eventful. We ended up taking in a stray dog and I woke up in the middle of the night in bed on the balcony. There were 2 beds yet somehow I found myself squashed with the noise of crickets down my ear. I was fine sleeping inside but my friend was too hot.

We explored into the town the next day which reminded me of a huge indoor market. I picked the wrong place. Not because it looked like an indoor market but because of the steep hills. They were the only way to get to town and my legs were in agony. My friend is an explorer and I found it very difficult keeping up with them.

I didn't go back to the town after that; my body just wasn't up to it. I spent the next few days at the hotel. I found the sun very tiring so stayed indoors mostly, except 1 night when we went to explore the night life. My symptoms were sky high and I was keeling over in the corner wanting to go back to the hotel. The locals were offering me shots of alcohol left right and centre but I wasn't having any of it. I'd hardly drunk a thing but I stayed out knowing my friend was having a good time, plus they had the key to the hotel so I had little choice. I felt I was holding them back but what could I do? They went to explore a few more times but I wasn't up to it. I felt like a party pooper and realized I had made a mistake.

We had paid for 4 nights but had to leave the hotel room before midnight on the final night meaning we had nowhere to sleep as our shuttle back to the airport was in the middle of the night. My symptoms were getting worse and I became very impatient. I was aching, had nowhere to lie down properly, hungry with nowhere to eat and sensitive to the noise of others drunken conversations. I'd had enough and became quite difficult to be around.

I slept for the majority of the flight home. I'd never been so happy to get back if I'm honest. The reality was that my friend went back to work the next day whilst I was bedbound for the majority of that following week. I felt like death warmed up except I wasn't warm due to my temperature problems. That was the difference between the average healthy person and someone who has M.E. however only my mum saw how I was that week and everything carried on as normal. It took me weeks till I started to gradually improve again. The experience made me realize just how limited I was.

It was November time and I'd barely recovered from my holiday. My great great aunty who was 96 had been in and out of hospital for the most part of the year. She had no choice but to move to a nursing home. Me and my mum had the job of clearing out her flat. I was barely fit to leave the house, never mind clearing out a flat. She lived around 40 minutes away from where I am and again, I was the only one who could drive. There was a time limit and it had to be done in 2 weeks. This meant 2 40 minute drives and a whole day of clearing out at least 3 times each week.

We had to space it out on alternative days as my body couldn't cope with going over every day. It was a nightmare and she was a real hoarder. It didn't help much that I felt my efforts weren't appreciated despite the toll it took on my body.

The whole ordeal meant I couldn't do anything myself other than rest. It was even more of an effort than usual to do things like washing myself. I had to completely write off any hobbies I had for those 2 weeks and for several weeks after.

The days we didn't go I was having complete rest, mainly in bed. I was feeling very weak, painful, mentally exhausted and I'd barely had time to recover from my holiday.

It was mid November time and I had finally heard about the tribunal. Here is the letter that came through:

> *About your EMPLOYMENT SUPPORT ALLOWANCE appeal Your appeal will be heard on 06/12/2013 at our tribunal.*
>
> *Please make sure you arrive by 10:30. The appeal will be heard at this time, or as soon as possible after it. If you do not attend, the tribunal may decide the appeal in your absence.*
>
> *I have enclosed venue directions and information about the help that we can given with your expenses. Please bring the appeal papers with you when you come to the hearing. This is the set of papers relating to your appeal, which was sent to you, and your representative, if you have one.*
> *If you have any further*

evidence which you want the tribunal to see, please send it to me at least 7 days before the tribunal hearing. This will give the tribunal time to consider it with your other papers.

If you need to contact me, please quote your national insurance number which is at the top of this letter.

By time the letter was received on top of how ill I felt, it was a struggle getting everything together in time. I luckily had help from a Welfare Rights Advisor who went through every step with me thoroughly. I needed representation and was also waiting for a support letter from my OT. I was having cognitive difficulties and so my mum helped write the following letter:

Dear Sir/Madam,

With regard to your letter dated 8th November 2013. Would it be possible to re-arrange the date for the appeal for my son Barry John Evans (ESA allowance)? We are waiting for a letter of support from the OT treating Barry at hospital and this hasn't arrived yet.
Also, we have requested representation from the Welfare Rights Advisory Service and apparently they can only do

> *representations on Wednesday's due to their being a small department of only four people.*
> *So would it be possible to have a new hearing date, on a Wednesday so he can be represented, and to allow a little more time for us to receive further written support from the hospital which we can forward to yourselves in advance of a hearing.*

However, this was the disappointing reply:

> *Dear Ms Evans (Appointee)*
> *About your EMPLOYMENT SUPPORT ALLOWANCE appeal*
>
> *I received a request asking if your hearing that is planned for 6/12/2013 can be arranged for another day.*
> *The request for a postponement has been refused. The tribunal will consider your appeal at*

> *10:30 on 6/12/2013 as planned.*
>
> *Please add this letter and the enclosed postponement request to the papers you already hold. Please note that the Tribunal can decide the appeal even if you do not attend the hearing. If you need to contact me, please quote your reference number which is at the top of this letter.*

I tried calling my OT daily for 2 weeks and the phone was answered once saying they weren't available but they'll pass the message on. I never heard anything back and had to attend the tribunal with no representation and no support letter. I began to wonder if it was even worth going. All I had were the following notes that the Welfare Rights Advisor helped me with:

> *Always use stick/crutch*
> *Balance affected and is worse first thing am*

Unable to manage 50 metres repeatedly, if at all

On a bad day I avoid walking as it is too painful

On a good day I can go out but am still limited to 50 metres before

Constant pain in legs mainly and also the arms if using a keyboard repetitively. Need complete rest.

Due to exhaustion/discomfort I need regular lie downs to stop the pains going worse.

At times, the pain is too severe and would avoid doing repetitively.

Sometimes my arms/fingers and hands and too painful and stiff

Takes a lot longer to process instructions step by step and need to run through repeatedly. There have been previous struggles but my ability has worsened since I've had M.E. Fatigue, memory problems and focusing mean

Feel overloaded, overwhelmed

These were brief notes to help as it was likely my brain fog would kick in. It wasn't a lot and the whole thing was very daunting. It felt like an Apprentice Interview where they try to catch you out. I was being asked questions at a fast pace and my mind couldn't keep up with it. It was very formal, uncomfortable and intimidating.

I was sat outside waiting for the decision and was adamant that the appeal would be lost. "What would I do if I wasn't fit for work?" This was just one of many questions/thoughts going through my head.

ESA Tribunal
DECISION NOTICE
1. *The appeal is allowed.*
2. *The decision made on 18/06/2013 is set aside.*
3. *Mr Barry Evans is entitled to Employment and Support Allowance ("ESA") with the work-related activity component.*
4. *This is because insufficient points were scored to meet the threshold for the Work Capability Assessment, but regulation 29 of the ESA Regulations 2008 applied.*
5. *No Schedule 3 descriptor applied.*
6. *The Tribunal recommends that the Department does not reassess until 12 months from today.*

I was relieved more than anything when the decision was made. I was handed a piece of paper with the above written on but nothing was explained to me. I found out at a later date that I had to attend a Work

Related Assessment Group which baffled me. However, it was a massive weight off my shoulders and I felt I could have a relaxing Christmas.

It was Christmas time, a time where people can relax and enjoy some quality time with their loved ones. For me however, I feel it's such a difficult time. Friends expect you to go out more and lots more is happening as the majority of people get time off work. I made the effort to go to a few things and as a result my body suffered.

Christmas Day and the surrounding days were some of the worse I'd ever had M.E. wise. I was pretty much bedbound. I hadn't missed a Christmas Day church service in years but I just wasn't up to going to this one. I spent the majority of it in bed fully clothed with my electric blanket on full. I was sweating but so cold at the same time, a horrible feeling.

New Years Eve is the night you can't miss, I really wasn't up to going but felt I couldn't let my friends down yet again. I'd already been out for a meal the week before but this was the night everyone was waiting for. To see in the New Year with your friends when it reality, I'd have been happier just to spend it at home relaxing. I spent the whole morning and most of the afternoon in bed before I went out. I didn't handle alcohol very well and I wasn't convinced I was going to be spending time with people who thought I was genuine.

In many ways it was an eventful night. Things got a little rowdy early on and I ended up hitting my head on the side of the sofa though the most hurtful part of the night was the part I should have enjoyed most. The countdown had arrived and most were a little worse for wear. When people are drunk you find out what they're really thinking. It wasn't nice having derogatory comments thrown at you when you're so fatigued and by that point that I was in no fit state to be getting into an argument. What causes these people to say such things? Well, you could blame for government for doing very little to raise awareness for M.E. but then you could also blame those who thought like this for being incredibly narrow-minded. It's also a vicious circle, if I'm not up to explaining my illness for the millionth time then how else are they going to know? From an outsider's point of view, M.E. is a very strange illness; in fact it's a very strange illness for those who have it too.

You could say man up but then why should I spend what little energy I have going out drinking when I don't really enjoy it anyway? Those days have been and gone for me. I could never imagine doing all nighters in Liverpool again like I had done a few years before. After how I was struggling over the Christmas period I found this all incredibly hurtful.

Ever since that night I have remained tee total. I had thought about it for a while and decided to put my health first seeing how I felt the next day. Alcohol was making me feel worse despite not often having it. I decided that I wasn't going to put myself out for others as much as I used to. I'd never drink alcohol for the pleasure of drinking it. That one night set me back a whole week.

I'd improved gradually over the Christmas period though have had my setbacks. This is mainly because I've took a different approach, maybe a slightly selfish approach but an approach that will be more beneficial to me in the future.

Chapter 5: Looking to the Future

It was a year since I'd been diagnosed with M.E. and it was sad to compare myself to last year. Back then I was mild, now I am moderate. I felt limited a year ago but now I was even more limited. If I leave the house at all during a week then it's deemed to be successful. If I have just 1 nap during the day then it's deemed to be successful. I have deteriorated but have to remain positive.

It didn't help that I had the worry of the Work Related Assessment Group coming up. My 1st meeting was very awkward, it was bound to be. I was clearly unfit for work yet found myself having to look at possible jobs I could do, it didn't make sense. I remember my advisor suggesting I went to my GP and asked to be put on a specific course to help get my "fitness" back up to scratch, I was told that I could see a Personal Trainer. I'd never heard of anything so ridiculous in my life. I didn't know which was more ridiculous, the fact that this was even suggested or the fact they actually knew I was a Personal Trainer myself. The meeting ended shortly after that and I was told to return for an appointment to update my C.V. I already had an up to date C.V. but they were running out of ideas of what to do with me. After all, it wasn't their fault; they were just doing their job.

I asked my OT for a report so I could show these people I was being genuine. Luckily this time I received a letter of support. It read as follows:

> *16th April 2014*
> *TO WHOM IT MAY CONCERN*
> *Barry was diagnosed with Chronic Fatigue Syndrome, (CFS/ME), by Dr M B on 10/01/2013. He attended a group information session on 12/06/2013 and following assessment on 6/09/2013 has begun to attend for individualised therapy sessions comprising of one to one visits, therapy telephone calls and workshops.*
> *The sessions provide information on*

pacing, grading activity, ordering sleep patterns and use cognitive behavioural therapy skills to explore personality factors. Beginning with an evidence based medical explanation of CFS/ME symptoms. Barry will be encouraged to learn and apply strategies and address life style issues that could be perpetuating the condition.

Research has shown that although there is no evidence of pathology in CFS there is evidence of severe cardiovascular and muscular deconditioning, circadian desynchroncisation with sleep disorder and increased nervous system arousal. In line with NICE guidelines, (August 2007), the strategies provided by the CFS Therapy Service form the building blocks of stabilisation, improvement and for some recovery.

If appropriate, patients generally receive up to twelve months input but are not expected to have recovered within that time. Statistics show an average recovery period of between two to five years, with therapy, for two out of three patients. Not all patients however will reach full recovery, or may relapse due to other medical diagnoses, events or difficult circumstances.

Barry has advised me that he has been advised to take part in whole-day workshops to support him in returning to work. I can confirm that as part of Barry's input from the service, we are looking at gradually increasing his activity, as per the National Institute of Clinical Excellence (NICE) 2007 guidelines for CFS/ME. The aim of these increases is to work towards a return to work in the long-term. Increases in activity outside of those monitored and supported by a health professional experienced in CFS/ME are not recommended, and are likely to cause increases of symptoms that will delay Barry's recovery. Barry is currently unlikely to be able to attend any work related activity for longer than an hour without experiencing additional symptoms. I would ask that you take this into account when making recommendations.

Be aware that a patient's progress can be impeded by returning to employment or training before they are ready. Increased stress during this vulnerable time will impair physical, mental and social function. As his advisor you should ensure you fully understand this complex condition when assessing entitlement. I hope you can take these points into consideration. Please find enclosed relevant information but I would encourage you to contact the service on the above number for more advice on the condition.

Barry's limitations of fatigue, pain, poor concentration and memory are entirely genuine and I would ask you to take them into account when assessing and offering support with Employment and Support Allowance. I draw your attention to the Disability and Equality Act 2010.

I was incredibly grateful for this letter of support. I felt it hit the nail on the head and I couldn't have asked for anything better.

Though much to my dismay, that report wasn't good enough and apparently not individual enough. They want to know by what date I will be recovered by but it just doesn't work like that. It's an ongoing situation that to be honest is going round in circles but once I'm well enough, I can hopefully work for myself and not have to worry about anything like this in future.

After reading the last few chapters, you probably wonder why I don't die of boredom. M.E. is incredibly debilitating and reduces our activity levels significantly. I've done my best to remain positive and I've adapted my lifestyle in many ways. I've also found new hobbies which I may never have discovered previously.

Music:

It has always been a dream of mine to be

able to sing and I felt that if I didn't do anything about it now then I may never get the opportunity. I have a singing teacher who visits me every couple of weeks for an hour. It's very helpful as I don't have the struggle of leaving the house and it's given me a new found love. I started having lessons around summer time 2013 and literally couldn't sing to save my life. I was as good as tone deaf; I was very pitchy and knew very little about the whole thing. Although I may not be able to practice as much as I'd like, I have made improvements and have grown to love music. I can now sing in tune which is a good start. I have an ambition to write my own material and it's something I feel really positive about. I also purchased a keyboard with the help of my grandfather who used to be a music teacher. I'm lucky to get 10 minutes practice a day in but it's an option I have for when I'm feeling up to it. The same as singing, I hadn't a clue about playing the keyboard and although the progress has been slower than the singing, I'm determined to improve.

My top three inspirations are:

1. Adam Lambert – An incredible vocalist who has amazing control over his instrument. He has a classical background and very rarely hits a bum note. I would go as far as saying that he's the most talented singer in contemporary music today.
2. Rhydian – He's always been an inspiration since he appeared on the x-factor. I've seen him perform at the Echo Arena in Liverpool and also The War of the Worlds and Rocky Horror and he stood out amongst everyone vocally.
3. Freddie Mercury – Speaks for itself, very talented singer who always put on a show. He died the year I was born but I take lots of inspiration from his many performances and albums he released.

You can see there's a pattern: vocally immaculate and flamboyant. I've discovered a whole variety of new music that I may never have found out about if I hadn't made the move to find a singing teacher. I have a new found love for 80's hair metal, progressive metal, and glam rock amongst many other genres. My guilty pleasure is the 80's metal scream which is a tough skill to master and also very energy consuming. I have a PA system to help me practice and had I not become ill, I may never have truly found a passion for music.

Theology:

As a devout Christian, it's always been an aim of mine to improve my biblical knowledge so I decided to enroll on a distance learning course in Theology. I pay per module and can take as long as I like to complete it; my 1st module took me nearly a year to complete but its small steps at a time. It keeps my brain active though it's extremely hard at times trying to study when you're having cognitive difficulties daily. It's certainly helped me spiritually and it's made me feel like I'm not at a complete stand still. Of course I want to recover from M.E. but I'm always looking at little things that can help to keep me progressing in various things that aren't too energy consuming.

Animals:

I'm a big fan of animals. They're loyal, understanding, loving amongst many other things so they're great company for me when I'm housebound. At the time of writing this book, I live with 14 and that's not including my mum or my brother.

Katy is a Shih Tzu dog aged 12. We've had her since she's been a puppy and she's a great companion. She often sleeps on the end of my bed at night.

Nancy, King, Smokey and Zoe are all cats. I bought Nancy as a Christmas present for my mum over two years ago, King came from a friend who became allergic to him, Smokey came to us as he was no longer safe where he was living due to his brother being poisoned, and Zoe is a kitten who randomly turned up on our doorstep one Saturday evening.

Daisy, Lucy and Twinkle are rats. They're incredibly misunderstood and out of all the animals I have a special bond with these the most and in particular Twinkle. She sits on a chew and uses it as a bus stop to wait for me at certain times of day and likes to sleep in my hood. They're all very affectionate and have some very individual characteristics.

Harvey is a giant rabbit who came to us on Christmas Eve a few years back. He's the same size as Katy and gets very grumpy when he doesn't get his own way. He doesn't show much emotion but he's a content creature.

Malcolm is a guinea pig. He was adopted a couple of years ago from a pet shop as his little buddies were bullying him. He lived with Bullwinkle for a while who sadly passed away last year. Malcolm has slowly adapted to life without a fellow companion.

Holly and Fleur are normal sized rabbits who stick to each other like glue. Harvey doesn't like Holly so they come out at different times.

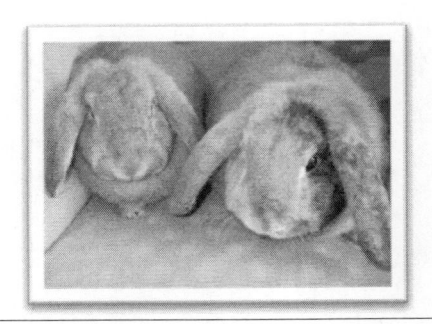

Dixie and Alfie are budgies. They're kept away from the cats for obvious reasons. Dixie has already lost two friends, Pixie flew away and Bluebell died. Alfie can't fly but he's content.

Blogging/Writing:

I'd never have dreamt of writing a book before but here I am writing this.

I also like to blog from time to time about different subjects such as M.E., Animals, Theology, Personal Training, Football and Music.

I also like to make Youtube videos and am learning bit by bit how to edit videos and add different features.

I find it sometimes helps to get my thoughts out on paper.

However hard it may be and however few they may be, if you dig deep enough then are things to be positive about. Keeping positive is essential for an illness like M.E. as it can be very easy to become de-motivated as you're so limited when it comes to everyday activities. I'm grateful I've been able to stick at these things despite the amount of setbacks I've had and may experience in the future.

Many people with M.E. have lead busy lives prior to getting a diagnosis. Motivation is usually something that has never been a problem in the past but the physical symptoms can make it very hard to keep going at times. Finding small hobbies I don't have to commit myself to have helped me greatly in coping. It's not ideal but it's the best for someone in my situation.

It can be very discouraging when looking at statistics like many M.E. sufferers lose around 80% of their friends on average, life expectancy can be shortened by 25 years, only around 5% of sufferers make a full recovery, sufferers are more prone to heart problems and so on.

Worry makes our symptoms worse, I've started meditation to try and eradicate the stress. I'm young and was previously very active, I didn't choose to have this illness yet I find myself housebound for long periods. I do still attend Cognitive Behavioral Therapy occasionally but if I'm honest, it feels more like I'm seeing a psychologist. I've got my physical symptoms under control and my OT feels I'm doing everything right and being set small tasks each time I attend, my tasks that to be honest I would be doing anything without the help from an OT.

Life adjustments have had to be made, there's no way around it. I've heard of people trying to continue to live their previous lives and they end up a lot worse off for it. There are many negative aspects to this illness but positives can be made.

I'm a stronger person now than I've ever been before. I've had some not nice experiences but they've all made me into a stronger person. If none of this had happened, I'd probably have remained a very shy and anxious individual who is afraid to express himself.

Have I become selfish?

I've always been a very honest guy. A guy who likes to put others before him and a guy who genuinely cares about others.

However, one thing I have learned since having M.E. is that sometimes you have to be selfish and put yourself first. If you keep putting yourself out to please others then it's putting your health at risk.

Is this being selfish or is it just merely showing concern for your own health? As a sufferer, of course it's the latter. However, an outsider may well choose the former.

This is what gives us a great dilemma, do we risk our health and keep friends or do we do what's best for our health and risk losing friends and family? It's easier said than done but the obvious answer would be that true friends will stick by you no matter what.

I've had many dilemmas and it takes a strong character to make these decisions. You have to become incredibly thick-skinned to survive with an illness like M.E., the phrase "like water off a ducks back" comes to mind when referring to negative comments.

For anyone reading this that has M.E., you are not being selfish. Health always comes first and true friends and family will realize that.

Positive thoughts

Circumstances are not ideal but you have to make the most of them. I've taken this opportunity to explore new things I may never have experienced when fit and healthy, for example my new found love for music. I'd never have contemplated writing a book if I'd been well either.

Physically, I'm in the worst shape I've ever been. I'm not overweight but compared to my former self I'm out of shape. As a Personal Trainer, I'm constantly looking at new ways I can try to add some form exercise into my routine. I've tried a few things that haven't worked but I'm constantly searching, with caution. Exercise isn't recommended with M.E. so I try very gentle exercises and having the knowledge of how the body works helps that. Very often I fail performing any form of exercise at all, but its little steps. It's also incredibly frustrating having to nap at certain times each day knowing that if I don't then I will get payback.

Using an appointment diary has been helpful, planning each day and what I do at different times can be beneficial but your life can become a bit of a ritual with no flexibility. They can be good when you have a busy period coming up but general pacing has worked best for me so far.

It pains me that I only get to leave the house a couple of times a week on average; I try to sit out a bit in the back yard each day to get that fresh air the body needs. Or face should I say as I very rarely just wear t-shirts anymore due to my cold body temperature.

I've always liked the idea of moving into my own place and being independent but if I'm completely honest, I'd find it extremely hard to cope on my own as the easiest of chores can prove to be too much at times.

I know that statistics prove that very few sufferers of M.E. return back to their former lives but I'm slowly adapting my life and exploring possible ways I can earn an income despite being ill. I plan on working for myself. It's an unrealistic short-term target to get back into the Personal Training so I'm looking at how I can provide my services online, I've purchased a domain name and written a few articles on fitness so I'm looking to make something of that. Who knows where my singing will take me? If I've come a long way since I started then there's no reason for me not to improve further. Of course, practice isn't always daily as my illness fluctuates but short bursts of singing will help to prevent my body from crashing out. Music wise, I'm working towards my grades in singing and piano which is something else I can do at my own pace. My theology course is keeping my mind active and is another small step towards achievement though achievement can sometimes mean surviving.

I don't smoke, I don't drink, I don't take

drugs and I have a very strict diet that I follow. I'm constantly looking at new healthy options for my diet as certain foods don't go down as well as others. My body is intolerable to certain things and is certainly intolerable to alcohol. I'm lucky I was never a regular attendee at parties as I've found cutting down completely on all these things relatively easy. I used to like the odd cigar but even that is proving too much for me at this time.

A useful piece of advice I've been given is to control the M.E. and not to let it control you. It's very easy to give in when our bodies are so weak, feeling like you've constantly got the flu but then there's a fine line between controlling the M.E. and being foolish. Pushing yourself to the point of crashing out is foolish. This can often be the case when you're having a better day. You feel like everything needs to be done in that one day and get excited you have a bit of energy, it's easy to do but can potentially make us worse. I've learned from just a short period of time that pacing is the way forward. There is no cure for

M.E., the only way forward is pacing. Other factors can help to relieve symptoms but the single best thing I've found that helps is pacing. It takes a lot of trial and error but once I'd mastered how much pacing my body needed and for how long, it helped me greatly. It's not always convenient to pace but I try the best I can.

I've done some incredibly stupid things in the past and not always had the chance to apologize so this is my way of doing it. I have the odd blip but such is life. This is a new chapter in my life and "A New ME".

Finally, a massive thank you to everyone who has taken the time to read this book and I genuinely hope that you can take something from this.